TUDOR AND STUART CHRONICLE

Contents

Tudor and Stuart Times	2
The Tudors	**4**
Henry VII, 1485-1509	4
Henry VIII, 1509-1547	6
The Great Harry, 1514	6
The Field of the Cloth of Gold, 1520	7
Henry VIII's divorce, 1533	8
The break with Rome, 1534	9
The end of the monasteries, 1536	10
The Great Bible, 1539	11
Edward VI, 1547-1553	12
Lady Jane Grey	13
Mary I, 1553-1558	14
Elizabeth I, 1558-1603	16
Sir Francis Drake	18
Sir Walter Raleigh	19
Mary Queen of Scots	20
The Spanish Armada, 1588	22
The Early Stuarts	**24**
James I, 1603-1625	24
The Gunpowder Plot, 1605	25
King James's Bible, 1611	27
Charles I, 1625-1649	28
The quarrel between King and Parliament	28
The Civil War	**30**
The siege of Corfe Castle, 1643-46	30
The course of the war, 1642-45	32
Prince Rupert	33
The battle of Naseby, 1645	34
The Republic and the Restoration	**36**
The execution of Charles I, 1649	36
The Republic, 1649-60	37
The battle of Worcester, 1651	37
Oliver Cromwell, Lord Protector, 1653-58	38
The Restoration, 1660	40
Charles II and his Times	**42**
The Royal Society	42
The Great Plague, 1665	44
The Great Fire of London, 1666	46
Index	**49**

Tudor and Stuart Times

About five hundred years ago a powerful family, the Tudors, started to rule in England. They were followed by another powerful family, the Stuarts. The Tudors and Stuarts ruled England for most of the sixteenth and seventeenth centuries. That is why the English often call them Tudor and Stuart times.

These were all rulers in the Tudor family.
The Tudors ruled England, Wales and Ireland.
Which Tudor ruled the longest?

Tudors	
Henry VII	1485-1509
Henry VIII	1509-1547
Edward VI	1547-1553
Mary I	1553-1558
Elizabeth I	1558-1603

At the time of the Tudors, the Stuarts ruled Scotland. After 1603 the Stuarts ruled England, Wales and Ireland too.
These were rulers in the Stuart family.

Early Stuarts	
James VI of Scotland and I of England	1603-1625
Charles I	1625-1649

There was no king or queen between 1649 and 1660.
This was because Britain was a Republic during those years.

The Republic	
Britain ruled by a Council of State	1649-1653
Oliver Cromwell, Lord Protector	1653-1658
Richard Cromwell, Lord Protector	1658-1659

These were also Stuart rulers. They ruled Britain after the Republic had ended.

Late Stuarts	
Charles II	1660-1685
James VII of Scotland and II of England	1685-1688
Mary II and her husband William III	1689-1702
Anne	1702-1714

Republic
A country without a king or queen whose rulers are chosen by the people.

In this book you can read about the kings, queens, lord protectors and other famous people of this time. You can also find out about the many important and exciting things which happened in Tudor and Stuart times, like the defeat of the Spanish Armada. The book is called a 'chronicle' because the events are in **chronological** order.

Chronological

In time order. The rulers of Britain on page two are arranged in chronological order.

In this picture the Spanish Armada is being set alight by the English ships outside Calais.

Most people did not take part in the big events of this time. What do you think life was like for them? Where did they live? What jobs did they do? You can find out about the lives of ordinary people in the book called *Tudor and Stuart Life*.

This picture shows women washing clothes in Tudor times

Roman Numbers

Roman numbers are usually used when talking about kings and queens.

V means five and I means one. Henry VII is Henry the seventh. Can you work out what the rest of the kings and queens should be called?

The Tudors

Henry VII, 1485-1509

Henry VII, he became king in 1485.

Elizabeth of York who Henry married in 1486.

In August 1485 two English armies faced each other at Bosworth Field in Leicestershire. One was led by the king, Richard III; the other by Henry Tudor, Earl of Richmond. Two hours later Richard was dead and his army defeated. His crown lay in a thorn bush where it had fallen. One of Henry's supporters picked it up and put it on Henry's head. Henry Tudor had become King Henry VII.

Richard belonged to the York family. Henry belonged to the Lancaster family. The leaders of these two powerful families had been quarrelling for thirty years about who should be King of England.

Henry made a promise before the battle of Bosworth Field. He said that if he won, he would marry Elizabeth of York and so unite the two families of Lancaster and York. What do you think Elizabeth might have thought about that? In 1486 he kept his promise. Henry and Elizabeth founded the Tudor line of rulers.

Henry VII chose this red and white double rose to be the special sign, or emblem, of the Tudors.

The white rose was the emblem of the York family. The red rose was the emblem of the Lancaster family. The wars they fought against each other are known as 'the Wars of the Roses'. Henry put the two roses together to show that the wars were over and that he stood for a united and peaceful country.

Here is Henry VII's **coat of arms** which included a red dragon, the emblem of the Welsh royal princes.

Coat of arms

'Arms' is an old word for badge. Knights used to have their arms on the coats which they wore over their armour. This told people who they were in a battle.

Find the red dragon. Henry was proud that he had a Welsh grandfather, Owain ap Meredith ap Tewdwr, and that he was born and brought up in Wales.

The Tudors

Henry VIII, 1509-1547

This is a painting of Henry VIII made in about 1536.

Henry VII died in 1509. His son became King Henry VIII. He was only seventeen years old. He was a good fighter. He rode horses well. He spoke French, **Latin** and Spanish, and he was a good musician.

> **Latin**
> Latin was the language of the Romans in ancient times.

The *Great Harry*, 1514

Henry spent a lot of money on the navy. He built forty-six large ships. This painting shows him on board his new flagship, known as the *Great Harry*. It was launched in 1514.

Find:

- the *Great Harry*. It is shown above the fort.
- Henry VIII. He is standing in the middle of the lower deck of the *Great Harry*.
- the fort. Henry quarrelled with the King of France and went to war. He built forts like this all along the south coast because he thought the French would try to invade. They were designed so that their guns could fire in all directions.
- the cannons. They were a new type of gun made of bronze.
- the soldiers going into the fort.

> **Bronze**
> A mixture of copper and tin.

The Tudors

The Field of the Cloth of Gold, 1520

Henry VIII thought it was important for a king to be surrounded by splendid things to show people how powerful he was. Here he is meeting the King of France, Francis I, in 1520. The event is known as 'the Field of the Cloth of Gold' because the Kings met in a tent made of gold cloth.

This painting shows several different scenes from the meeting.

Find:
- Henry and his procession (bottom left).
- a pretend palace specially built for Henry (bottom right). It had a brick base, wooden walls and real glass in the windows.
- the Kings meeting in the tent of gold cloth (top centre).
- fighting on horseback, called 'jousting' (top right).
- a dragon firework let off by the English (top left).

The Tudors

Henry VIII's divorce, 1533

Henry VIII was married to a Spanish princess, Catherine of Aragon. They had several children but the only one to survive was a girl called Mary. Some people thought a woman could not be the **monarch**. Why do you think that was? Henry was very worried. He wanted a boy to succeed him but Catherine was too old to have any more children.

> **Monarch**
> A king or queen.

Catherine of Aragon, daughter of King Ferdinand and Queen Isabella of Spain. She was very popular in England.

At the same time Henry fell in love with a young woman called Anne Boleyn. He decided to divorce Catherine and marry Anne. He hoped he and Anne would have a son.

The **Church** did not allow people to divorce. Kings could sometimes divorce their wives if the **Pope** gave them special permission. Henry VIII asked the Pope for permission to divorce Catherine. The Pope said 'no'.

In 1533 Henry decided to divorce Catherine without the Pope's permission. Then he married Anne Boleyn. After all the fuss, Anne had a baby girl. They named her Elizabeth.

> **Church**
> The Roman Catholic Church. In Henry's time everyone in England belonged to it.

> **Pope**
> The head of the Church. He lived in Rome.

Anne Boleyn. Her marriage to Henry VIII lasted only three years. In 1536 they quarrelled and she was executed. Henry had six wives. This is who they were and what happened to them:

- Catherine of Aragon — married in 1509 — divorced in 1533
- Anne Boleyn — married in 1533 — beheaded in 1536
- Jane Seymour — married in 1536 — died in 1537
- Anne of Cleves — married in 1540 — divorced in 1540
- Catherine Howard — married in 1540 — beheaded in 1542
- Catherine Parr — married in 1543 — still married to Henry when he died.

The break with Rome, 1534

Now that Henry had disobeyed the Pope he had to make sure the Pope could not punish him. So in 1534 he made himself head of the Church of England. That meant the Pope in Rome could no longer tell him what to do. This event is known as 'the break with Rome'.

This picture shows Henry VIII taking over the Pope's power in England.

Find:
- Henry VIII on his throne.
- the Pope under Henry's feet.
- the priests trying to help the Pope.
- the man beside Henry handing him a book. This is Thomas Cranmer. Henry made him Archbishop of Canterbury, the chief bishop of the Church of England. He helped Henry to divorce Catherine and break away from Rome.

Why do you think Henry VIII wanted pictures like this to be made?

What do you think the Pope might have thought about it?

Bishop

A bishop is the priest in charge of all the priests and churches in a big area. His own church is called a cathedral.

The Tudors

The end of the monasteries, 1536

In Henry VIII's time monasteries and nunneries, where monks and nuns lived, were very rich places. You can find out more about the lives of monks and nuns in *Tudor and Stuart Life*.
In 1536 Henry ordered the monasteries and nunneries to be closed and he took over all their lands and riches.

He closed them because he badly needed money to pay for soldiers and forts to defend England. The Catholic King of Spain, Charles V, was angry about the way Henry had treated the Pope. Henry expected Charles to attack England at any moment.

The ruins of Rievaulx Abbey in North Yorkshire. Most monasteries gradually fell to bits after Henry closed them. What clues are there that this monastery was once very wealthy?

The Tudors

The Great Bible, 1539

In Henry VIII's time all Church services were in Latin. Priests understood Latin, but most people did not. Henry wanted everyone to know more about the teachings of the Church so he asked a priest called Miles Coverdale to translate the **Bible** from Latin into English.

This new English Bible was called the 'Great Bible'. In 1539 Henry ordered it to be printed. One copy was placed in every church.

> **Bible**
> The book containing the Christian holy writings.

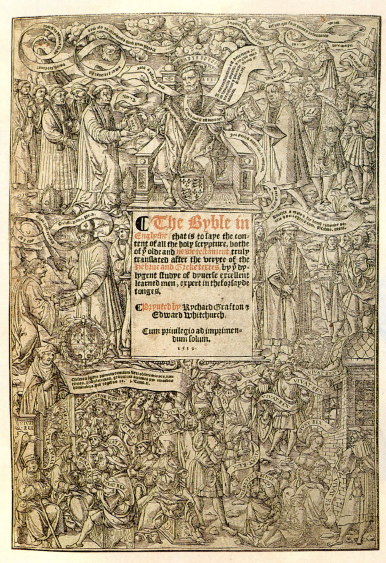

The first page of the Great Bible of 1539. A much smaller version, for people to read at home, was printed in 1540.

Edward VI, 1547-1553

When Henry VIII died his nine year old son, Edward, became king. Edward's mother was Jane Seymour whom Henry married in 1536.

Edward was well educated and clever. Although he was very young he held strong opinions. This picture was painted to show his ideas about religion.

Edward was a **Protestant**. Protestants did not agree with the teachings of the Catholic Church and refused to obey the Pope.

Edward told everyone to use a new **Prayer Book** which Archbishop Cranmer wrote in English. He also said priests in the Church of England could marry. The Catholic Church does not allow priests to marry.

Find:

- Edward VI on his throne.
- Henry VIII in his sickbed pointing at Edward to show he wants him to be king.
- the men sitting at the table. Henry asked them to help Edward rule until he was old enough to rule on his own.
- soldiers outside breaking down Catholic religious statues.
- the Pope being crushed by an English Bible.

Protestant
The word 'protestant' means someone who protests or argues against something. People who wanted to change the Catholic Church were called Protestants because they were protesting against it.

Prayer Book
A book of church services and prayers.

Lady Jane Grey

In 1553 Edward VI fell ill and it was obvious he was going to die. The Duke of Northumberland, Edward's chief adviser, was very worried. Henry VIII's **will** said that if Edward died without children his half-sister Mary, daughter of Henry VIII and Catherine of Aragon, should be the next monarch.

The Duke knew that Mary was a strong Catholic. He was afraid she would punish him for helping Edward.

The Duke tried to save himself with a clever plan. He persuaded Edward to make a will of his own saying that Lady Jane Grey should be the next monarch. Lady Jane was related to Henry VIII. She was also a Protestant.

> **Will**
> A written paper that tells people what you want done with your belongings after you have died.

When Edward died the Duke of Northumberland announced that Jane was now queen. He sent soldiers to capture Mary, but she escaped and demanded to be made queen herself. Many important lords supported Mary so the Duke gave himself up. He asked for mercy, but Mary had him executed. Lady Jane was sentenced to death and executed the following year.

Lady Jane Grey. She reigned for nine days, but was never crowned queen.

The Tudors

Mary I, 1553-1558

Mary I. She had an unhappy childhood after Henry VIII divorced her mother, Catherine of Aragon. She lived apart from both of them in various royal palaces. Her father hardly ever saw her and refused to let her see Catherine.

Mary was a Catholic. She ordered everybody to stop using the English Prayer Book and to go back to the old services in Latin. Many people were pleased. They liked things the way they had always been.

Mary found that one priest in every ten was married. She changed the rules again and said priests could not be married. Married priests had to leave their wives or else stop being priests. Many priests and their wives found it difficult to decide what to do. Why do you think that was?

Mary also said the Pope was to be head of the English Church again. She apologised to the Pope for what Henry VIII had done.

Some people were now Protestants. They did not want to go back to the old Catholic services and they refused to obey the Pope. Mary believed it was her duty to punish them. She ordered Protestants to be arrested and burnt to death in public.

The burning of two Protestant Bishops, Latimer and Ridley, in 1555. They had helped Edward VI.

Find:
- Latimer and Ridley.
- the bundles of firewood, called 'faggots'.
- the men sitting down. They were in charge of the execution.
- the priest preaching to the crowd.
- the soldiers.

Burning was a normal punishment in those days for people who refused to follow their ruler's religion. In other countries Protestant rulers had Catholics burnt if they refused to change their beliefs. Even so the burnings were very unpopular in England.

Mary's marriage was unpopular too. Most people wanted her to marry an Englishman and have a son who would become king when she died. Mary said she wanted to marry a Spaniard, Prince Philip.

The English did not like this idea. They knew Prince Philip would one day become King of Spain. That meant England might come under Spanish rule. Mary refused to listen to their objections. She married Philip in 1554, but he spent most of his time in Spain.

Mary did not have the child she wanted so much. She died in 1558, a sad and lonely woman.

Prince Philip of Spain. In 1556 he became King Philip II of Spain.

Elizabeth I, 1558-1603

Mary's successor was her twenty-five year old half-sister Elizabeth, daughter of Henry VIII and Anne Boleyn. Elizabeth was lucky to be alive. The five years of Mary's reign were a dangerous time for her.

Princess Elizabeth aged about fourteen, shown with her books. She learnt the ancient languages of Latin and Greek as well as Italian, French and Spanish. She also studied history, geography, mathematics, science and music. She enjoyed dancing and hunting.

Elizabeth was a Protestant. She had been very careful when Mary was queen. She went to Catholic church services. Mary did not believe Elizabeth was truly a Catholic, but she could not prove anything.

Even so Mary ordered Elizabeth to live under guard in a royal house in Woodstock near Oxford. Later she allowed Elizabeth to live normally again in her favourite palace in Hatfield.

Hatfield House where Elizabeth spent much of her childhood. She was staying here in 1558 when she heard the news that Mary had died and she was now queen.

Because Elizabeth was a Protestant she wanted nothing to do with the Pope. She became head of the Church of England herself. She brought back services in English. She tried to make the services please as many people as possible, but many Catholics were unhappy with the new Church and refused to go to its services.

Elizabeth had this picture painted soon after she became queen. After all the troubles of Mary's reign, she wanted to remind people that she was Henry VIII's daughter and to tell them she would rule as well as he did.

Find:

- Henry VIII with Edward VI kneeling next to him.
- Elizabeth hand in hand with a figure who stands for peace and wealth.
- Mary and Philip of Spain with a figure in a helmet who stands for war.

What do you think Elizabeth wanted people to think about Mary?

Why do you think Elizabeth and Edward are shown on one side of Henry while Mary is shown on the opposite side?

Sir Francis Drake

Sir Francis Drake was a famous sailor in Elizabeth's reign. Between 1577 and 1580 he sailed round the world. He was the first person from Britain to do this.

Like most English sailors Drake hated the Spaniards. The Spaniards had conquered peoples and lands in South America. They found gold and silver there. But they would not let anyone else share it.

Drake planned to capture Spanish treasure ships and steal the gold and silver they were taking back to Spain. Find their route on the map below.

He worked out that the best way to surprise the Spaniards would be to attack their ships in the Pacific Ocean. He left Plymouth with five ships. He reached the Pacific with only one left, his flagship, the *Golden Hind*. Follow his voyage on the map.

Drake and his sailors captured an unarmed Spanish treasure ship carrying so much gold and silver that it took them six days to put it all into the *Golden Hind*.

To stop Drake going back to England, Spanish ships blocked the Straits of Magellan. Find the Straits on the map.

Drake decided the best way home was to sail west. Follow his route on the map.

When he arrived in London, Queen Elizabeth was so pleased with him that she made him a knight.

Sir Francis Drake. Why do you think he is shown with his hand on a globe?

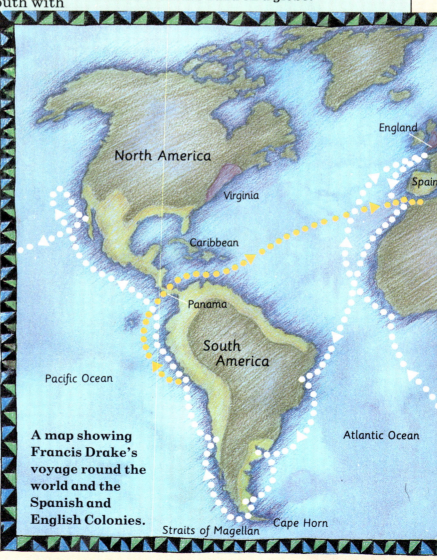

A map showing Francis Drake's voyage round the world and the Spanish and English Colonies.

The Tudors

Sir Walter Raleigh

Sir Walter Raleigh was one of Elizabeth's favourite **courtiers**. He was a soldier, a sailor and a clever talker and writer. He wrote many poems praising the Queen.

Raleigh knew that the Spaniards had found gold and silver in America. He wanted to do the same. In 1585 he paid for settlers to go to a part of North America which he named Virginia. Find it on the map.

A year later the settlers had disappeared, we do not know what happened to them. Perhaps they quarrelled with the people who lived there and were killed. Perhaps they died in the cold winter.

The first English people to settle successfully in Virginia went there in 1607. You can find out more about this in *Tudor and Stuart Life*.

Courtiers

People from important families whose job was to be with the king or queen at all times. Some helped to rule the country. Some helped to organise the royal household. Some were people the monarch particularly liked to have as companions.

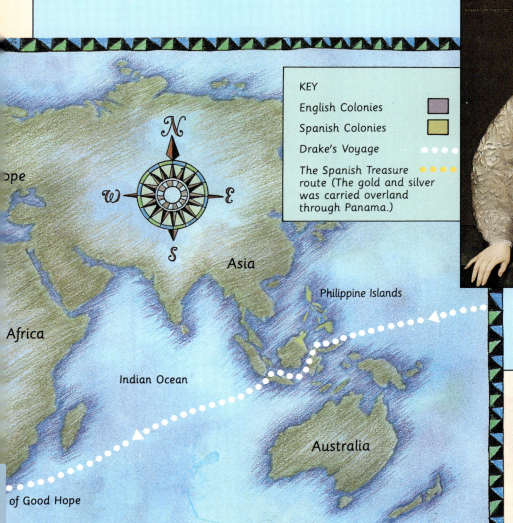

KEY
English Colonies
Spanish Colonies
Drake's Voyage
The Spanish Treasure route (The gold and silver was carried overland through Panama.)

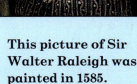

This picture of Sir Walter Raleigh was painted in 1585.

19

The Tudors

Mary, Queen of Scots

This is Mary Stuart who became Queen of Scotland in 1542 when she was only six years old. She was too young to rule on her own so a Scottish lord ruled as **regent** for her. Her mother, who belonged to an important French family, took her to live in France.

When she was eighteen Mary went back to Scotland. She was a strong Catholic, but while she was away the Scottish lords had set up a Protestant Church. Mary promised not to change it.

The Scots wanted Mary to marry and have a child who could be king or queen after her. In 1565 she married Lord Darnley. They had a son, James, but Darnley was not a good husband.

One night an explosion wrecked the house in Edinburgh where he was staying. Darnley and a servant were found dead in a nearby garden. They had been strangled. The sketch below was made at the time and shows the scene.

> **Regent**
> Someone appointed to rule on behalf of a king or queen who is too young or too ill to rule themself.

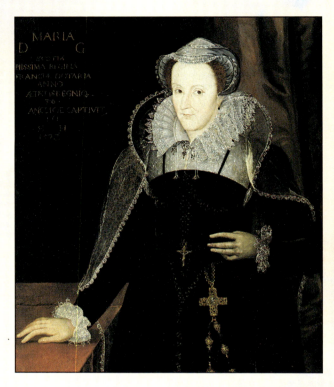

Mary Stuart, Queen of Scotland. She was also known as Mary, Queen of Scots

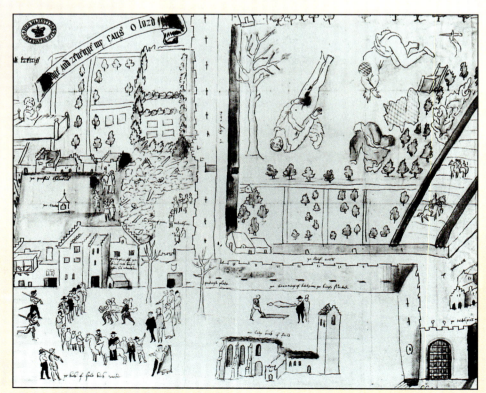

Find:
- the bodies of Darnley and his servant.
- the remains of the blown-up house in the middle.
- the bodies being carried away and buried.

By this time Mary was in love with another lord called the Earl of Bothwell. Everyone said Bothwell had murdered Darnley. Mary organised a trial that found Bothwell not guilty. Then she married him.

The Scots did not like this. They forced her to give up the throne. James became king. Mary escaped to England and asked Elizabeth I for help.

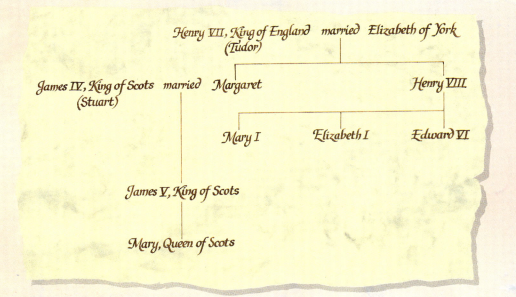

How the Tudors of England and the Stuarts of Scotland were connected.

You can see from the diagram that Mary was next in line to be Queen of England as long as Elizabeth had no children. As soon as Mary arrived in England, English Catholics plotted to kill Elizabeth and make Mary the queen.

Elizabeth was advised to have Mary executed. Elizabeth kept her under guard for twenty years, but refused to order the death of another monarch. Then spies proved that Mary herself was trying to have Elizabeth killed. Elizabeth gave way. Here is Mary being executed at Fotheringhay Castle in 1587.

Find:
- the special stage built for the execution.
- the onlookers.
- Mary, Queen of Scots.
- people burning her clothes after her death.

The Spanish Armada, 1588

Philip II of Spain wanted England to have a Catholic king or queen. He decided to invade England, get rid of Elizabeth and put a Catholic monarch in her place. He ordered an armada, or great fleet, to be built.

Use the map to follow Philip's plans. He wanted the Armada to sail along the English Channel to pick up soldiers from the Spanish Netherlands where he had an army. The Armada was to take the soldiers across to England to capture Margate and then to conquer the rest of the country. Do you think it was a good plan?

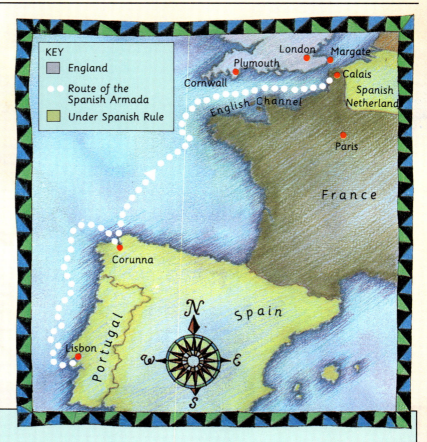

Crescent

The shape of the new moon.

The Armada left Spain in the summer of 1588. On 30th July English lookouts on the cliffs of Cornwall saw the sails of the Spanish ships. The English fleet was in Plymouth harbour when the Armada arrived. This chart, made shortly afterwards, shows what happened next.

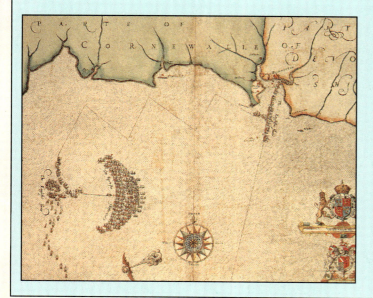

That night the English fleet managed to sail against the wind and get into position behind the Armada.

Find:

- the route taken by the main part of the fleet commanded by Lord Admiral Howard and Sir Francis Drake. It sailed across the front of the Armada and then round behind it.

- the route taken by the rest of the fleet along the coast of Cornwall and then behind the Armada.

- the Spanish Armada sailing in the shape of a crescent. The Spaniards put their strongest ships at each end. Why do you think this made the Armada very difficult to attack?

The English and Spanish ships were about the same size and each side had just over a hundred fighting ships. The English attacked the Armada as it sailed along the English Channel.

It anchored at Calais and the Spanish Admiral, Medina Sidonia, sent a message asking if the soldiers in the Netherlands were ready. They said they needed another six days. This painting shows what happened next.

The English took eight ships and filled them with things that would burn. They set them alight and let them drift into the Spanish fleet. The Spanish captains had to sail away quickly to stop their wooden ships catching fire.

Then the English attacked. The battle lasted six days. Eight large Spanish ships were put out of action as well as many smaller ones. More than a thousand Spanish sailors were killed.

Suddenly a strong wind blew the Armada to the north. It could not sail back to the Netherlands. Medina Sidonia ordered it to sail home round the north of Britain.

The English were lucky. They had run out of food and ammunition. In the end it was the wind that saved them.

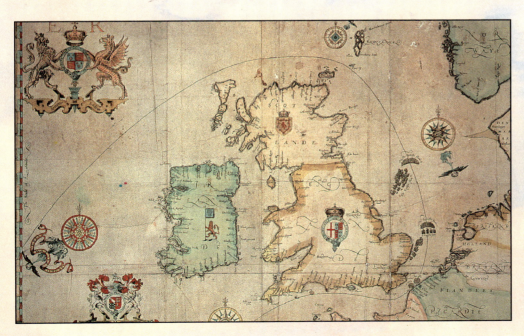

This map, made at the time shows the route of the Armada. On the way home many Spanish ships were wrecked on the coast of Ireland.

The Early Stuarts

James I, 1603-1625

Elizabeth I did not marry and had no children. On the night she died a messenger rode to Scotland to invite King James VI of Scotland, the son of Mary, Queen of Scots, to become King James I of England. England and Scotland now shared the same king.

James VI of Scotland, and I of England. He became King of Scotland in 1567 when Mary, Queen of Scots escaped to England.

The Early Stuarts

The Gunpowder Plot, 1605

James I was a Protestant and like Elizabeth I he wanted English people to belong to the Church of England. Elizabeth had made Roman Catholics who refused to go to Church of England services pay a large amount of money. Catholics hoped James would be less hard on them, but they were disappointed. Things stayed the same.

> **Parliament**
>
> Parliament met at Westminster Palace to advise the king or queen and help them make laws.
>
> In the House of Lords were lords and bishops. They met in the Parliament House.
>
> In the House of Commons were members elected by landowners and wealthy towns' people. They met in St Stephen's Chapel.

In 1605 this group of Roman Catholics tried to kill James and his chief advisers. Their plan was to blow up the House of Lords while the King was inside opening **Parliament**. It has been known ever since as the 'Gunpowder Plot'.

The gunpowder plotters. They were all men from important families who owned large amounts of land, except Bates who was a servant. How does the artist show this? The artist drew this after the plot. What do you think he wanted people to think about the plotters?

The Early Stuarts

The plotters' first idea was to tunnel under the House of Lords from a house nearby. Things went well until they found themselves up against the stone foundations of the Parliament House. They had to give up.

Then they managed to hire a cellar right underneath the House of Lords. They hid thirty-six barrels of gunpowder there. Guy Fawkes was given the job of setting it off at the right moment.

A few days before the opening of Parliament a lord called Mounteagle received this unsigned letter. It warned him not to attend the ceremony. Mounteagle showed the letter to Robert Cecil, the King's chief **minister**. Cecil showed it to James who decided there was a plot and ordered the Parliament House to be searched.

> **Minister**
> Someone who helped the king or queen to govern.

The letter sent to Lord Mounteagle. One sentence says 'I say they shall receive a terrible blow this Parliament, and yet they shall not see who hurts them.' James I decided that meant gunpowder. Later he said God helped him to work it out.

Guards found Guy Fawkes in the cellar and arrested him just before midnight on 4th November. He was carrying this lantern and slow burning matches to light the gunpowder.

Guy Fawkes's lantern. You can see it today in the Ashmolean Museum, Oxford.

No one is sure who wrote the warning letter to Lord Mounteagle. Robert Cecil said one of the plotters wrote it to save Mounteagle's life. Most of the plotters knew Mounteagle well because he was a once a Catholic. He had recently changed to become a Protestant.

Historians think Cecil knew about the plot all along. Guy Fawkes refused to say who the other plotters were. He only gave their names when he was tortured. But two days before that Cecil ordered them to be arrested. That means he already knew their names.

Perhaps Cecil told his spies to watch the plotters and arranged for them to be discovered at the last minute. He probably wanted to turn people against Catholics. If so, he succeeded. Many people feared Catholics for more than a hundred years because of the Gunpowder Plot. The plot itself is still remembered every 5th November on Bonfire Night.

The execution of the plotters in January 1606. This drawing was made nearly two hundred years later.

King James's Bible, 1611

James I wanted a new English translation of the Bible to be made. The job was given to forty-seven scholars working in teams. Each team worked on a particular section of the Bible. It took them three and a half years. Their translation, sometimes known as 'King James's Bible,' was printed and published in 1611.

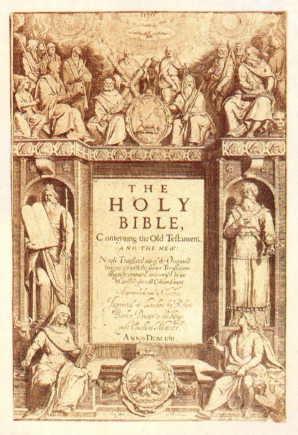

The title page of King James's Bible.

Charles I, 1625-1649

When King James died, his son Charles became King Charles I of Scotland and of England. Here is Charles I and his wife Henrietta Maria.

Charles loved the services and ceremonies of the Church of England. He disagreed with people called **Puritans** who wanted plain and simple services. Puritans accused him of wanting to bring back the Catholic religion.

Henrietta Maria was the daughter of the King of France. She was a Catholic. Charles allowed her to have her own Catholic priest at court. What do you think people thought about that?

Puritans

Puritans did not like priests to wear special robes because it reminded them of the Catholic Church. They thought it was important to read and discuss the bible and listen to sermons. They chose to wear plain, rather than fashionable, clothes.

The quarrel between King and Parliament

By Charles I's time many members of the House of Commons were Puritans. They used meetings of Parliament to criticise the King. Charles thought he knew what was best for the country. He decided to rule without Parliament's help.

He was allowed to do this, but he was supposed to ask Parliament if he needed extra money to run the country. For eleven years Charles found ways of raising money without asking Parliament.

When he called Parliament again its members were angry. They made Charles promise to call a Parliament every three years and never again to raise money without its agreement.

The Early Stuarts

The leader of Parliament was a Puritan gentleman called John Pym. Pym did not trust Charles to keep his promises so he tried to take away even more of the King's power. He said Parliament, not the King, should be in charge of the army. Charles was furious. Why do you think Pym said that? Why do you think it made Charles so angry?

Charles accused Pym and four of his friends in the House of Commons of **High Treason**. He took some soldiers to arrest them. Someone warned Pym and the five slipped out of a back door as the King arrived. Here they are getting into a boat to escape down the River Thames.

High Treason
The crime of being an enemy to your own king, queen or country.

This picture was painted for the House of Commons about two hundred years later. Why do you think members of Parliament wanted this picture painted?

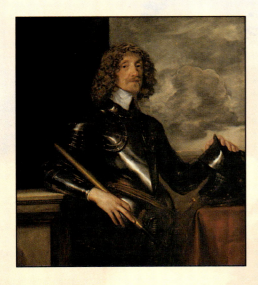

This is Sir Edmund Verney. He supported the King. His son, Sir Ralph, supported Parliament. Sir Edmund became the King's standard-bearer. He was killed at Edgehill, the first battle of the Civil War, in 1642.

Some people in Parliament supported the King and some supported Pym. They could not settle their argument by talking. They formed armies and so a **civil war** broke out. People had to decide which side to support. Sometimes members of the same family supported opposite sides.

Civil war
A war fought between people living in the same country.

The Civil War

The siege of Corfe Castle, 1643-46

This is Corfe Castle in Dorset as it looks today. At the time of the Civil War it was the home of Sir John and Lady Bankes. Sir John was an important judge. He supported the King in the war and spent most of his time in Oxford where Charles I had his headquarters.

The Civil War

In 1643 Parliament's soldiers started a **siege** around Corfe Castle. They used guns to try to knock down the walls. Then they used ladders to try to climb over the walls.

The attack on Corfe Castle in 1643. Look at this picture and the one opposite showing Corfe Castle today.

Which parts of the castle are still there?

Which have gone?

Siege

A way of attacking a town or castle by surrounding it so that no one can get in or out. The idea is that in the end those inside will run out of food, and surrender.

This is Lady Bankes who defended the castle with the help of her maids and a few soldiers. They heaved stones over the walls to stop the attackers climbing the ladders. In the end the attackers went away.

The next year they were back, but Lady Bankes managed to hold out until 1646. By then the King had lost the war and in the end Lady Bankes surrendered. Parliament ordered the castle to be destroyed and most of it was blown up. That is why it is a ruin today.

The course of the Civil War, 1642-45

The Civil War started in 1642 and ended in 1646 with the defeat of the King. Look at the maps to see how the armies of the King and Parliament gained and lost parts of England each year. You can see that the King's armies did well in the first two years, but Parliament's victory at Marston Moor in 1644 gave it control of the whole of the north of England. The following year Parliament won the battle of Naseby and after that took over most of the country.

1643

Areas controlled by King and Parliament, 1643

KEY
- area held by Parliament
- area held by the King

1642

Areas controlled by King and Parliament, 1642

KEY
- battle
- area held by Parliament
- area held by the King

These maps show you the parts of England controlled by the King's armies and the parts controlled by Parliament's armies in each year from 1642 to 1645. In which year did the King control the most land?

The Civil War

1644

Areas controlled by King and Parliament, 1644

KEY
- battle
- area held by Parliament
- area held by the King

1645

Areas controlled by King and Parliament, 1645

KEY
- battle
- area held by Parliament
- area held by the King

Cavalry
Soldiers who fight on horseback.

Prince Rupert

This is Prince Rupert, Charles I's nephew. He came from Germany to fight for Charles. He commanded the King's **cavalry**. He was a brave fighter and won victories for two years until he was defeated by Parliament's cavalry at the battle of Marston Moor, near York, in 1644. Rupert escaped from the battlefield. It is said he hid in a beanfield to avoid being captured.

The Civil War

The battle of Naseby, 1645

In 1645 Parliament created a new army called the 'New Model Army'. Its soldiers were well drilled and well paid. Its commander was a Yorkshire gentleman called Thomas Fairfax. Oliver Cromwell, a gentleman from Huntingdonshire and a member of Parliament, was in charge of the cavalry. You can read more about the New Model Army in *Tudor and Stuart Life*.

In the same year the New Model Army won its first battle, at Naseby in Northamptonshire. This picture was drawn shortly afterwards. It shows the two armies facing each other just before the battle.

The Civil War

The battle of Naseby.

Find:
- the King's army at the top of the picture.
- the New Model Army.
- the village of Naseby.
- the villagers watching.
- guns.
- foot soldiers carrying pikes or muskets.
- Prince Rupert's cavalry on the right of the King's army.
- Oliver Cromwell's cavalry on the right of the New Model Army.

After Naseby the King ran out of money and could not pay for another army.

The Republic and the Restoration

The execution of Charles I, 1649

After the Civil War Parliament's leaders accused Charles I of making war on his own people. They said the bloodshed and misery was all his fault. A special court tried him and sentenced him to death. In 1649 Charles I was executed outside the Palace of Whitehall in London.

Charles is shown twice on the scaffold, once alive and once dead.

The Republic, 1649-1660

After the execution of the King, Parliament said there were to be no more monarchs and it abolished the House of Lords. England became a **republic** ruled by Parliament and a **Council of State**. Here is Parliament's seal, or stamp, for 1651, showing its members at work.

> **Republic**
> A country whose rulers are chosen by the people.

> **Council of State**
> A group of people chosen from Parliament to run the day to day business of the country.

The battle of Worcester, 1651

After 1649 the Royalists were still strong in Ireland and Scotland. Oliver Cromwell was put in charge of the New Model Army with orders to defeat them. First he went to Ireland and then, in 1650, to Scotland where Charles I's son, Prince Charles, had been crowned king.

Cromwell defeated the Scots. Then Charles led an army into England. Cromwell followed him and defeated him at the battle of Worcester in 1651. Charles managed to escape to France. These pictures, drawn at the time, show his adventures after the battle.

Find:
- the battle of Worcester.
- Charles hiding from Cromwell's soldiers in an oak tree.
- Charles riding to Bristol, disguised as a servant to a lady called Jane Lane.
- a ship taking Charles to France from Shoreham in Sussex.

Oliver Cromwell, Lord Protector, 1653-58

This is Oliver Cromwell. In 1653 he went to Parliament with a band of soldiers and sent the members away. He and the other officers in the army said that Parliament was ruling badly.

Oliver Cromwell painted after 1653 when he was Lord Protector. He became a member of Parliament in 1628. He was a very successful cavalry officer in the Civil War. He was a member of the court that tried the King and ordered his execution. In 1649 he became commander-in-chief of the New Model Army.

The army officers made Cromwell ruler instead. He was called 'Lord Protector'. He ruled with a Parliament. Its members came from England, Wales, Scotland and Ireland.

Cromwell was a Puritan who wanted a Church in which all Protestants (but not Catholics) could hold the type of services they pleased. This was unusual. Most rulers in Cromwell's time wanted everyone to believe in exactly the same things.

Cromwell never managed to put his ideas into practice. Too many people were frightened of them. They thought that if ordinary people were allowed to hold their own services, they would soon stop doing as they were told by their landlords and the people they worked for.

Cromwell enjoyed poetry, music and dancing. Forty-eight violinists and fifty trumpeters played at his daughter's wedding and the dancing went on past midnight and into the early morning.

He did not approve of the sort of pastimes shown here. He tried to stop people gambling, swearing and playing games on Sunday.

The cover of a book about how to play games, first published in 1674. Games like these became very popular after the end of Puritan rule in 1660.

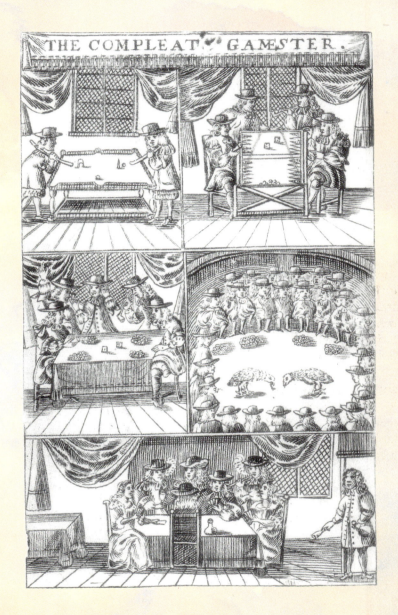

Cromwell was ruler only because he commanded the army. The army officers agreed with his ideas, but most people did not want to be ruled by soldiers. In 1657 Parliament suggested that Cromwell should become king. Then he would have to rule according to the laws. The army officers did not like this idea, so Cromwell refused the offer.

The Restoration, 1660

This is Richard Cromwell, Oliver's son, who became Lord Protector when his father died in 1658. Richard did not want to be a ruler and had no idea what to do. The army officers persuaded him to resign. They called back the members of the Parliament that Oliver Cromwell had sent away in 1653.

Most people were fed up with being ruled by soldiers. They preferred to be ruled in the old way by a king or queen and a Parliament of Lords and Commons.

In 1660 Parliament invited Prince Charles to come home and become King Charles II. This event is called the 'Restoration' because a monarch was restored or brought back again as ruler.

The House of Lords was also restored, and so was the Church of England which Parliament had abolished in the Civil War.

Here is Charles II's coronation procession. Most people were happy to see the splendid processions and ceremonies of the monarchy back again.

Find Charles II. He is the tall figure in a hat on a white horse.

The Republic and the Restoration

Charles II wanted to bring people together again after the splits caused by the Civil War and the time of the Republic. He pardoned everyone who had fought against his father except those who had condemned him to death in 1649. He invited people from both sides in the Civil War to advise him and help him rule.

Cromwell's wife, his son Richard and his daughters were allowed to live in peace. But people burnt figures of Cromwell on bonfires in London and in 1661 his body was dug up and hanged on the anniversary of Charles I's death. Afterwards his skull was put on a spike.

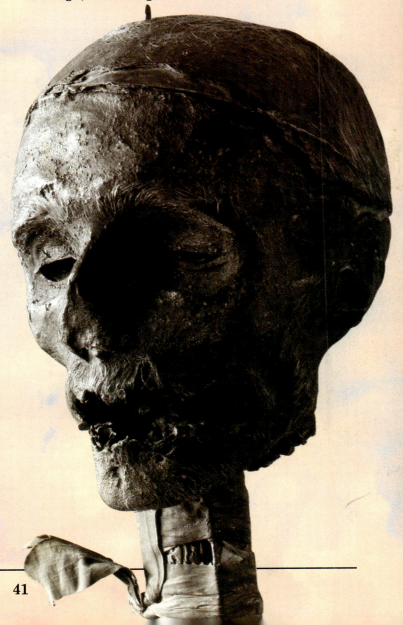

Cromwell's skull on the spike. It was found in recent times and is now buried in Sidney Sussex College, Cambridge.

Charles II and his Times

The Royal Society

During the time of the Civil War and Republic a group of scientists started to hold meetings to discuss their ideas. In 1660 they decided to ask Charles II for permission to form a special society. The King agreed and, because he was interested in science and inventions, he said he would become its **patron**. The society was named the 'Royal Society'. This portrait shows Charles as Patron of the Royal Society.

Find:
- the ships. Charles was especially interested in inventions to do with ships.
- the telescope.
- the globe of the stars on the table.
- the globe of the earth under the table.

Patron

Someone who helps and protects a person or a group of people.

The Royal Society helped scientists talk to each other about their ideas and learn from each other. Its members made many discoveries. A scientist called Robert Hooke used a microscope like this one to look at very small things and find out how they were made.

Microscopes were invented in about 1650. Telescopes were invented earlier in around 1600.

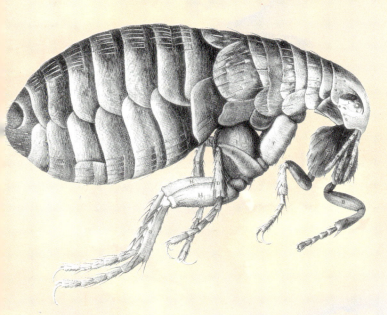

Hooke's drawing of a flea under a microscope made in 1665.

This is the mathematician Sir Isaac Newton, probably the most famous member of the Royal Society. In 1687 he worked out that a force which he called 'gravity' causes things thrown up in the air to fall back to earth. He worked out that gravity also affects the way planets move in the heavens.

Up until then many people believed the earth and the heavens were completely separate worlds and worked according to different rules. Newton showed they were part of the same universe and worked by the same rules.

The Great Plague, 1665

In 1665 people all over the country died from a disease which they called the 'plague'. The plague broke out quite often in Tudor and Stuart times, but the outbreak in 1665 was the biggest one of all. About a hundred thousand people died. That is why it was called 'the Great Plague'. Some people in London called it 'the poor's plague' because better-off people left the city leaving the poorest people behind.

Here is a drawing of a London street during the plague. As soon as someone was found to have the plague their house was shut up and no one was allowed to leave it. A red cross was painted on the door to warn people. Someone called a 'watcher' stood outside to see that no one left the house.

Find:

- the crosses on the doors.
- the watchers outside. Houses had to stay shut up for forty days after the person with the plague had died or recovered.
- the women with sticks. They were called 'searchers'. Their job was to look at the bodies of everyone who died and find out if they had died of the plague.
- two men carrying a box on poles. This is called a 'sedan chair'. A person sat on a chair inside the box. The men are probably taking a sick person to a place called a 'pest house' outside the city.
- the man chasing the dog. The Lord Mayor ordered all dogs and cats to be killed. Some people thought they carried the plague germs.

So many people died that special pits, like these, had to be dug for the bodies. People called 'corpse bearers' went through the streets at night calling, "Bring out your dead". They put the bodies on carts and took them on carts to the pits.

This is a costume worn by doctors to protect themselves from the plague. They thought germs lived in air that smelled nasty, so they stuffed the beak on the front with herbs and spices to make the air they breathed smell sweet and keep the germs away.

The plague germs really lived in fleas which, in turn, lived on black rats. The rats lived among the dirt and rubbish that was all over London's narrow streets. After 1665 black rats began to die out. They were killed off by brown rats which did not carry the plague fleas. So there were fewer and fewer outbreaks of plague after 1665.

The Great Fire of London, 1666

On 2nd September 1666 a fire broke out in a baker's shop in Pudding Lane, in London. A strong wind caused the fire to spread. The houses in London were built mainly of wood and were very close together.

A man called Samuel Pepys watched the fire spread and described it in his diary:

> 'As it grew darker, the fire appeared more and more, in corners and upon steeples, and between churches and houses as far as we could see up the hill of the City'.

Soon the sky was lit up with the flames. The red glow could be seen in Oxford more than fifty miles away.

This painting by a Dutch artist shows the fire at its fiercest.

Find:

- the castle on the right. That is the Tower of London which was not burnt.
- the large church in the centre. That is the old St Paul's Cathedral which was burnt down.
- people escaping with their belongings. Some are in boats on the River Thames.

Charles II took command of the fire-fighting and ordered sailors to blow up houses to make spaces, which the fire could not cross. After three days the fire began to die down.

Over thirteen thousand houses and eighty-seven churches were destroyed. Pepys went to see the damage. The ground was so hot it even burnt the soles of his shoes. He wrote:

> 'The people who now walked about the ruins appeared like men in some dismal desert.'

Outside the city in the fields of Islington and Highgate he saw more than two hundred thousand people lying by the heaps of things they had managed to save from the fire.

After the fire an architect called Sir Christopher Wren built this tall column so that people would remember the Great Fire. You can still see it in London today. It is called the 'Monument' and stands not far from the baker's shop where the fire began.

A drawing of the Monument. It also shows a new kind of water pump that was invented to help put out fires in the future.

Sir Christopher Wren was also given the job of building fifty-two new churches in place of the ones that had been burnt down. In 1673 he began the job of building a new St Paul's Cathedral.

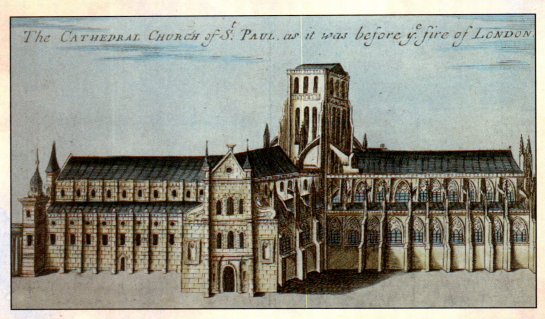

This is the old St Paul's just before it was burnt down in the fire. It once had a spire, but it fell down.

This is the new St Paul's, designed by Wren, which still stands today.